AF485916

ORACLE 1Z0-339 EXAM PRACTICE QUESTIONS

Exam Practice Questions & Dumps for Oracle 1Z0-339

Presented By: Emerald Books

About Emerald Books:

Emerald Books is a publishing house based in Hudson, Texas, USA, a platform that is available both online & locally, which unleashes the power of educational content, literary collection, poetry & many other book genres. We make it easy for writers & authors to get their books designed, published, promoted, and sell professionally on worldwide scale with eBook + Print distribution. Emerald Books was founded in 2015, and is now distributing books worldwide.

QUESTION 1
You have deployed a new SOA Composite. As part of one of the customers
use cases, they want you to allow all users to withdraw their requests made
through self-service console.

Select the correct statement.

A. A request can be withdrawn during any stage of the process. A request
   can be withdrawn before the Operation Initiated stage. Only admin users
   are able to withdraw ongoing requests.
B. A request can be withdrawn during any stage of the process. A request
   can always be withdrawn by a requester only, which is done by using
   Identity Self Service.
C. A request can be withdrawn before the Operation Initiated stage. A
   user's managers are the only ones able to withdraw employee requests.
D. A request can be withdrawn before the Operation Initiated stage. Only
   admin users are able to withdraw ongoing requests.
E. A request can be withdrawn before the Operation Initiated stage. A
   request can always be withdrawn by a requester only, which is done by
   using identity Self Service.

QUESTION 2
Your customer reports that several users submitted self-registration

requests and those entries are shown as auto approved. Identify the

reason.

A. Default Home Organization Policy is disabled.
B. SOA Server is off.
C. Default Home Organization Policy has been deleted.
D. Two or more Home Organization Policies are overlapping.

QUESTION 3
You are running an upgrade from Oracle Identity Manager PS2 to PS3. As
part of the deployment of the workflow orchestration service, you must set
up two components from the system administration console.

Select the two system values to be changed (Choose two.)

A. set SOA Workflow Enabled as TRUE
B. set SOA Workflow Policies Enabled as TRUE
C. set Workflow Disabled as FALSE
D. set Workflow Policies Disabled as FALSE
E. set Workflow Enabled as TRUE
F. set Workflow Policies Enabled as TRUE

QUESTION 4
A company wants to provision access to conference rooms using OIM. The
reservation should contain the start and end date of the reservation, the
name of the conference room, and the location code.

Which three steps are required to Implement a Disconnected Application
Instance for Conference Room access provisioning based on the previous
description? (Choose three.)

A. Create a Sandbox in OIM Administration Console.
B. Create a Sandbox in OIM Self Service Console.
C. Create a Form to represent a Conference Room Reservation.
D. Create a Disconnected Application Instance named "Conference Room
    Reservation".
E. Modify the Form generated by default when creating the Disconnected
    Application Instance.
F. Add a child form for the reservation entitlements.

QUESTION 5

A user has a resource that was provisioned via an Access Policy. Then the

user is added to a role that denies the resource via another Access Policy.

Select the option that describes OIM's expected behavior.

A. The resource will be denied.
B. The resource will be allowed.
C. It depends upon the priority of the Access Policy.
D. This is a conflict and is reported at the time of adding the role to the user.

QUESTION 6

You are trying to set up session recording within Oracle Privileged Account Manager (OPAM) to record Windows sessions. You have deployed all of the correct components to the Windows server. However, when you try to test the target from the administrative console, you get the following error:

```
ConnectionFailedException: Unable to get the Directory
Entry
```

You have confirmed that the credentials in the target configuration are correct. What is the problem?

A. The Connector Server is not running on the target.
B. A firewall is blocking the connection from the OPAM server to the target.
C. The Windows server is a domain controller or joined to an Active Directory domain.
D. The administrator does not have permissions within OPAM to create a new target.

QUESTION 7
You are deploying Oracle Identity Governance. As part of one of the
implementation milestones, the customer wants to enable the certification
feature to enhance the compliance review process.

Which three tags must be set up through Design Console to generate
certification for entities? (Choose three.)

A. User_Key = true
B. Account_Status = true
C. AppInstance = true
D. UID = true
E. ITResource = true
F. AccountName = true
G. Entitlement = true

QUESTION 8
You are asked to set approvals for all role management tasks such as

creating and modifying roles.How will you achieve this in OIM 11g R2 PS3?

A. Select the Approval Required flag while defining a role.
B. Enable Identity Auditor features.
C. Select the Approval Required flag while defining access policy/
D. Define an approval policy.

QUESTION 9
Which two methods can be used to seed Identity Analytics warehouse?
(Choose two.)

A. using the Identity Audit Console
B. importing Identity feeds through federation standards
C. using seamless integration with Oracle Mobile and Social
D. using seamless integration with Oracle Identity Manager
E. importing Identity and Entitlements feeds by using ETL processing

QUESTION 10
You belong to the Retail organization, which is a suborganization of Product Development. The following configuration is in place In the Catalog:

1. The Account Manager, Customer Advocate, and Technical Support Agent roles have been created and published to the Product Development organization.
2. The Create Account, Remove Account, View Account Details, Submit Purchase Order, and Cancel Purchase Order entitlements have been published to the Retail, Manufacturing, and Public Sector organizations.

Select three correct statements about Catalog searches performed by you (Choose three.)

A. You will not see any of the roles published to the Product Development organization.

B. You will see all roles and entitlements published to the parent organization to which her organization belongs.

C. You will not see any of the entitlements published to the Retail organization because they have not been published to the Product Development organization.

D. You will not see any roles but will see all the entitlements as per the described configuration.

E. You will not see any roles published to the Product Development organization unless the "Include Sub-Orgs" check box was selected when the roles were published to it.

QUESTION 11
An organization requires that all the requests for Catalog Items be approved
by the Catalog Item Administrator, which is defined as a Custom Metadata
Attribute of Catalog Items.

Which are the four configuration and customization steps required to
achieve this functionality? (Choose four.)

A. Create Approval Workflow Rules to configure the customized SOA
   Composite as the Approval Process for the requested resources.
B. Customize the Human Task to route the requests to the Login ID of the
   Catalog Item Administrator of the requested resource.
C. Add Custom Metadata Attribute to hold the Login ID of the Catalog Item
   Administrator.
D. Create a managed bean to do the routing of the request to the proper
   target user.
E. Customize the SOA Composite used for Approvals to invoke OIM APIs
   for the Catalog to extract the Login ID of the Catalog Item Administrator
   from the Catalog Item's metadata.
F. Create one or more Approval Polices to configure the customized SOA
   Composite as the Approval Process for the requested resources.

QUESTION 12
Identify the type of action that needs to be performed in order to execute an
identity audit policy along with its associated rules against a given
population of entities.

A. Identity Audit Scan
B. Identity Remediation
C. Identity Policy Violation
D. Identity Rule Condition

QUESTION 13
You are customizing Self-Service capabilities. You have been requested to

create a rule for temporary users that allows them to add roles to their own

profiles only. Select the correct code fragment that enables such behavior.

A. If user.Profile Equal TempUsers THEN capability rule addRoles
B. If user.Role Equal TempUsers THEN capability Equal addSelfRoles
C. If user.Role Equal TempUsers THEN capability rule selfModifyUser
D. If user.Profile Equal TempUsers THEN capability rule selfModifyRoles

QUESTION 14
Which report contains information on temporary access that even if granted
may not be appropriate or justified in the long term?

A. Certified Access Report
B. Abstained Access Report
C. Certified Conditionally Access Report
D. Certified Temporary Access Report

QUESTION 15
A company is using a Disconnected Application Instance to represent
Conference Room Reservation. There is a new requirement of having the
list of attendees along with their email addresses, and a list of equipment
items to be provided for the meeting.

Which three tasks should you perform to implement this requirement?
(Choose three.)

A. Create a Child Form for the Equipment Items provided for the meeting
    and configure it as an Entitlement form.
B. Create a Sandbox in Administration Console.
C. Modify the parent form to add multivalue attributes to hold the attendees
    and equipment items.
D. Create a Lookup code containing items of equipment that can be
    provisioned to a meeting in a given conference room.
E. Create a Child Form for the Equipment Items provided for the meeting.

QUESTION 16
Identify the correct statement about role consolidation.

A. It informs you that a role cannot be created.
B. It alerts you about other similar roles that already exist.
C. It alerts you about identical roles that already exist.
D. It informs you that a role does not have any members.

QUESTION 17
What is the global of the Oracle Web Services Manager (OWSM) policy
`oracle/multi_token_noauth_rest_service_policy`?

A. gets/modifies My Profile, Change My Password, and Change My
   Challenge Responses
B. creates HTTPS calls to the REST Interfaces
C. enforces OAM-OIM Authorization
D. secures SCIM resources

QUESTION 18
Identify two prerequisites for configuring Oracle Identity Manager Server
(Choose two.)

A. starting the OAM Managed Server
B. starting the SOA Managed Server
C. starting the Oracle WebLogic Administration Server for the domain in
   which OIM has been deployed
D. starting the OUD Managed Server

QUESTION 19
Which rule is seeded during Oracle Identity Manager initialization as part of
the default home organization policy?

A. All Users To Single Organization
B. All Users To All Organizations
C. Default All Users To Single Organization
D. Default All Users To All Organizations

QUESTION 20
What minimum level is required for attestation of form data for user profile
auditing?

A. None
B. Resource
C. Resource Form
D. Core
E. Process Task

QUESTION 21
Your customer has requested to deploy Oracle Identity Governance

certification service to enhance compliance processes.Which system

property must be set up to enable this feature?

A. OIM Certification Feature Set Availability set to ENABLE
B. Identity Certification Feature Set Availability set to ENABLE
C. OIAOIM Integration Feature Set Availability set to TRUE
D. Identity Auditor Feature Set Availability Set to TRUE

QUESTION 22
Which option must be enabled in Oracle Identity Manager to allow users to
complete certifications in offline mode?

A. Certification Offline mode
B. Offline Interactive Excel
C. Offline mode
D. Interactive Excel

QUESTION 23
The approval request for the Help Desk Rep role must go to multiple

people.How should you use the Catalog Item's metadata to fulfill this

requirement?

A. Set the Approver User to a list of users separated by commas.
B. Set the Fulfillment Role to the role containing the approvers of the
   request.
C. Set Provisioning Role to the role containing the approvers of the
   request.
D. Set the Approver Role to the role containing the approvers of the
   request.

QUESTION 24
A customer has requested a report listing any account existing in the
production environment that is also provisioned to the corresponding user in
OIM, but for which the process data does not match.

Which kind of report would allow you to show such data?

A. Orphaned Account Summary Report
B. Fine Grained Entitlement Exceptions By Resource
C. Rogue Accounts By Resource
D. Account Reconciliation Exceptions by Resource

QUESTION 25
As part of a new customer User ID life cycle improvement project, you have
deployed Oracle Identity Manager with Auditor mode enabled. They use
Oracle Unified Directory as their main LDAP repository.

Which Oracle component acts as the Identity Store for the solution
provided?

A. Oracle Access Manager
B. Oracle Identity Manager
C. Weblogic
D. Oracle Privileged Account Manager
E. Database
F. Oracle Unified Directory

QUESTION 26
As part of a company's new Identity Management strategy, you are
requested to enable OPAM's Microsoft Windows accounts support in order
to manage privileged account and record users activities.
The customer is unable to track ongoing sessions.Why is this happening?

A. You must install the OPAMAgentservice in the Microsoft Windows target
   to track ongoing sessions.
B. The Microsoft Windows session recording is only available in checkout
   history when the session has ended.
C. The Microsoft Windows "over-the-shoulder" capability must be enabled
   in the OPAM target configuration window.
D. You must register the OPAM agent in the Microsoft Windows target with
   the –r option: `OpamAgencUtility.exe -r`

QUESTION 27
A customer has requested that the OIM self-service UI be customized to
show their new logo. After running the customization, you are not able to
see the changes. The old logo still remains visible on the main page.

What is the reason for this?

A. As part of the customization process, during sandbox creation, the
    "Activate Sandbox" option was not selected.
B. The `commandImageLink` component was deleted.
C. The `commandImageLink` component binding property was set to
    `False`.
D. The `commandImageLink` component icon property is set as `NULL`.

QUESTION 28
Customer has upgraded their Oracle Identity Manager deployment from
PS2 to PS3.

What must be ensured from the approval workflow perspective during this
upgrade process?

A. Approval workflows replace the older approval policies structure. In an
    upgraded environment, you need to enable the use of newer approval
    workflow through the System Administration console.
B. Approval Policies replace the older approval workflows structure. In an
    upgraded environment, you need to enable the use of newer approval
    policies through the System Administration console.
C. Approval workflows work in tandem with the approval policies structure.
    In an upgraded environment, you need to enable the use of newer
    approval workflow through the System Administration console.
D. Approval workflows work in tandem with the approval policies structure.
    In an upgraded environment you need to enable the use of newer
    approval policies through the System Administration console.

QUESTION 29
Which two parameters from the User profile audit data collection level must
be set to none in order to disable auditing capabilities in Oracle Identity
Manager? (Choose two.)

A. `XL.UserProfile`
B. `XL.AuditDataCollection`
C. `XL.RoleAuditLevel`
D. `XL.UserProfileAuditDataCollection`
E. `XL.RoleAudit`

QUESTION 30
User1 has delegated `security_manager` privileges in OPAM to User2.

User2 wants to further delegate this access to User3 with read access

privileges only. How can User2 accomplish this task?

A. `security_manager` delegations are not allowed to further delegate
   access privileges to resource groups.
B. Log in to OPAM Console, click the resource, the Delegate tab, select the
   `user_manager` role and add User3 within the user list.
C. If the delegation is for `security_manager` privilege, User2 can only
   delegate `security_manager`.
D. Log in to OPAM Console, click the resource, the Delegate tab, add
   User3 within the user list and select the "Read Only" check box.

QUESTION 31
Your customer is deploying Oracle Privileged Account Manager as part of

their new security strategy. One of their requirements is to enable schema

encryption. Identify the script that needs to be executed to enable

encryption in the OPAM schema.

A. opamxencrypt.sql in IAM_HOME/opam
B. opamxencrypt.sql in IAM_ HOME /opam/sql
C. opamencrypt.sql in IAM_ HOME /opam/sql
D. opamencrypt.sql in IAM_ HOME /opam

QUESTION 32

Your customer requires an approval workflow rule that allows User Administrators with the beneficiary's organization to submit a request without initiating approval workflows.

Select the correct option that allows such behavior.

A. Rule Condition:
```
requester.adminroles CONTAINS OrclOIMUserAdmin
```

   Rule Outcome:
```
Direct
```
B. Rule Condition:
```
requester.adminroles CONTAINS OIMUserAdmin
```

   Rule Outcome:
```
Direct
```
C. Rule Condition:
```
requester.admin CONTAINS OIMUserAdmin
```

   Rule Outcome:
```
Indirect
```
D. Rule Condition:
```
requester.admin CONTAINS OrclOIMUserAdmln
```
   Rule Outcome:
```
NoApprovalRequire
```

QUESTION 33

Which two options represent correct statements about how Closed-Loop Remediation works by default? (Choose two.)

A. A revoke request coming from someone other than the user's manager can be challenged.
B. A revoke request coming from the user's manager can still be challenged.
C. After a revoke request is submitted in a review, the user can't do anything about it.
D. Only requests coming from the user's manager are auto-approved.
E. Because the revoke requests come from the Certification Process, they are carried out immediately.

QUESTION 34
You changed a role name by using Oracle Identity Self Service, However,

you realize that the User Profile Audit (UPA) tables in the database are not

updated. What should you do?

A. Nothing. The change will be shown during the next snapshot of the user.
B. Manually update the User Policy Profile data (UPD).
C. Disable the `XL.UserProfileAuditDataCollection` system property
   to allow changes through Self-Service Console.
D. Update role names through the UGP table only.

QUESTION 35
Which two statements are true regarding Identity Virtualization Library?
(Choose two.)

A. If the back-end LDAP server port is configured over SSL, then the
   Oracle Identity Manager user must use keytool to import the trusted
   certificate from the LDAP server into the Identity Virtualization Library
   keystore.
B. Identity Virtualization Library and Oracle Identity Manager are deployed
   on the same container.
C. Identity Virtualization Library can be installed on a separate server on
   which the directory server is installed.
D. Identity Virtualization Library and Oracle Access Manager are on the
   same container.

QUESTION 36
Which three features can be managed only by using the Oracle Identity
Manager Design Console? (Chose three.)

A. Forms Designer
B. Adapter Factory
C. Lookup Definitions
D. Process Definitions
E. Reconciliation Rules
F. IT Resource Definitions

QUESTION 37
Your customer has reported that the IT staff is not able to access a
Microsoft Windows privileged account through OPAM. According to them,
both OPAM and the Connector on the target system are properly
configured.

How should you access the Microsoft Windows server and enable the
logging in verbose mode?

A. Edit ConnectorServer.exe.config and add the following lines:
```
<switches>
        <add name="ActiveDirectorySwitch" value="3" />
</switches>
```
B. Edit ConnectorServer.exe.config and add the following lines:
```
<switches>
        <add name="ActiveDirectorySwitch" value="4" />
</switches>
```
C. Edit ConnectorServer.conf and add the following lines:
```
<switches>
        <add name="LocalAccountSwitch" value="5" />
</switches>
```
D. Edit ConnectorServer.exe.conf and add the following lines:
```
<switches>
        <add name=" LocalAccountSwitch " value="5" />
</switches>
```


QUESTION 38
You were requested to modify a Disconnected Application Instance and add
a child form to it. After making the modifications and publishing your work,
the child form doesn't appear in the request form.

What is causing this?

A. A Lookup Code for the new child form was not created.
B. The Regenerate View button was not clicked.
C. The custom child form was not saved.
D. The Catalog Synchronization Scheduled Job was not run.

QUESTION 39
Your customer reports that the IT staff is not able to update some OPAM
configuration resource objects through RESTful interfaces by using the
configuration resource API. They claim that they are trying to update the
number of Windows agents that have been deployed and that the
parameters sent are correct. However, they are not receiving a successful
message.

API Parameters

```
URI:
https://opam_server_host:opam_ssl_port/opam/config/sess
ionmgrconfigMethod: GET
Content-Type: NA
Body: JSON representation of Modification
```

What should you do to fix this?

A. Set the method as `POST`.
B. The `WindowsAgentCount` resource object can't be updated through
   the configuration resource API.
C. Set URI as
   `https://opam_server_host:opam_ssl_port/opam/config/se`
   `ssionconfig.`
D. Send `configUID` and `configType` along with the
   `WindowsAgentCount` parameter to run the update.

QUESTION 40
By default, the New User Registration facility is available from the login page

of the Identity Self-Service interface.How can you disable this behavior for

cases where identity creation is allowed only through reconciliation?

A. It can be controlled through the Access Policy configuration.
B. It can be controlled through the Approval Policy configuration.
C. It can be controlled through the System Configuration property.
D. It cannot be overridden, so you can remove the self-register link from
   the UI.

QUESTION 41

Your customer has deployed Oracle Identity Manager 11g PS3 and Oracle Mobile Security Suite as part of their new security and enterprise mobility strategy. They realize that both components are not working seamlessly.

Why is this happening?

A. The OMSS Enabled system value must be set as TRUE to enable OIM and OMSS integration.
B. The OMSS Disabled system value must be set as FALSE to enable OIM and OMSS integration.
C. The XL. IsOMSSEnabled system value must be set as TRUE to enable OIM and OMSS integration.
D. The XL.IsOMSSDisabled system value must be set as FALSE to enable OIM and OMSS integration.

QUESTION 42

The customer wants to extend one of their IT mobile applications. They are trying to pull out service account passwords through a REST API; however, they can't get that information.

These are the configuration parameters:

```
URI:
https://opam_server_host:opam_ssl_port/opam/target/{tar
getUID}/showpassword
Method: PUT
Content-Type: application/jsonBody: NA
```

What is the reason for this issue?

A. Content-Type must be set as `application/x-javascript`.
B. URI must be set to
   `https://opam_server_host:opam_ssl_port/opam/target/`
   `{targetName}/showpassword`.
C. The method must be set as `GET`.

D. This API is not available in Oracle Privileged Account Manager.

QUESTION 43

A company created a Catalog with items tagged with one or more of the following categories using the custom tags metadata attribute: Enterprise, Department, Team, and Project.

Select the option showing the code that builds the right CatalogSearchCriteria for a search that will correctly populate the Catalog search results with the list of Entitlements tagged with a selected category. Only Entitlements must be displayed.

A.
```
CatalogSearchCriteria tags = new
CatalogSearchCriteria
(Catalogsaarchcriteria.Argument.TAG,
selectedcategory,
CatalogSearchCriteria.Operator.EQUAL);
CatalogSearchCriteria cat = new CatalogSearchCriteria
(CatalogSearchCriteria.Argument.CATEGORY,
"Entitlement",CatalogSearchCriteria.Operator.EQUAL);
CatalogSearchCriteria scrt = new
CatalogSearchCriteria (tags,cat,
CatalogSearchCriteria.Operator.AND);
```

B.
```
Catalogsearchcriteria scrt. = new
CatalogsearchCriteria
(Catalogsearchcriteria.Argument.CATEGORY,
"Entitlement",CatalogSearchCritetia.
Operator.EQUAL);
```

C.
```
CatalogSearchCriteria        scrt       =        new
CatalogSearchCriteria
(CatalogSearchCriteria.Argument.TAG,
selectedCategory,  CatalogSearchCriteria.  Operator.
EQUAL);
```

D.
```
CatalogSearchCriteria tags = new
CatalogSearchCriteria
(CatalogSearchCriteria.Argument. TAG,
selectedcategory,
CatalogSearchCriteria.Operator.EQUAL);
CatalogSearchCriteria cat = new CatalogSearchCriteria
(CatalogSearchCriteria. Argument. CATEGORY,
"Entitlement",CatalogSearchCriteria.Operator.EQUAL);
CatalogSearchCriteria scrt = new
CatalogSearchCriteria (tags, cat,
CatalogSearchCriteria.Operator.OR);
```

QUESTION 44
As part of the deployment process, the CISO requires certification reports to be shown in the Detailed Information section of the Oracle Identity Manager Dashboard.

Which option within the Identity Self-Service Console must be configured?

A. Under Identity Audit, select Enable Certification Reports.
B. Under Identity Audit, click Identity Configuration and select Enable Certification Reports.
C. Under Configuration, click Certification Configuration and select Enable Certification Reports.
D. Under Identity Certification, click Certification Configuration and select Enable Certification Reports.

ANSWERS

1. Correct Answer: E
   Explanation/Reference:
   Reference
   https://docs.oracle.com/cd/E27559_01/user.1112/e27151/req_mangmnt_user.htm#OMUSG191
2. Correct Answer: B
3. Correct Answer: BE
4. Correct Answer: ADE
5. Correct Answer: A
6. Correct Answer: A
7. Correct Answer: EFG
   Explanation/Reference:
   Reference
   https://docs.oracle.com/cd/E37115_01/admin.1112/e27149/managecert.htm#OMADM5104
8. Correct Answer: D
   Explanation/Reference:
   Reference:
   https://docs.oracle.com/cd/E21764_01/doc.1111/e14316/auth_policy.htm#OMUSG823
9. Correct Answer: BE
10. Correct Answer: ACD
11. Correct Answer: CDEF
12. Correct Answer: A
    Explanation/Reference:
    Reference:
    https://docs.oracle.com/cd/E52734_01/oim/OMUSG/idaudit.htm
13. Correct Answer: B
14. Correct Answer: C
    Explanation/Reference:
    Reference
    https://docs.oracle.com/cd/E52734_01/oim/OMADM/workingrep.htm#OMADM226
15. Correct Answer: ABC
16. Correct Answer: C
17. Correct Answer: D
18. Correct Answer: BC
19. Correct Answer: C
    Explanation/Reference:
    Reference
    https://docs.oracle.com/cd/E52734_01/oim/OMADM/hmorgpol.htm#OMADM5578
20. Correct Answer: C
    Explanation/Reference:
    Reference

https://docs.oracle.com/cd/E27559_01/admin.1112/e27149/audit.htm#OMADM4762

21. Correct Answer: D
22. Correct Answer: D
Explanation/Reference:
Reference
https://docs.oracle.com/cd/E37115_01/admin.1112/e27149/managecert.htm#OMADM5081
23. Correct Answer: D
24. Correct Answer: A
25. Correct Answer: B
26. Correct Answer: D
27. Correct Answer: A
Explanation/Reference:
Reference
http://www.oracle.com/webfolder/technetwork/tutorials/obe/fmw/oim/oim_11g/simple_customization_OIM/Simple_Web_Customization.pdf
28. Correct Answer: A
29. Correct Answer: CD
Explanation/Reference:
Reference
https://docs.oracle.com/cd/E40329_01/admin.1112/e27149/audit.htm#OMADM3105
30. Correct Answer: B
31. Correct Answer: B
Explanation/Reference:
Reference
https://docs.oracle.com/cd/E37115_01/install.1112/e27301/opam.htm#INOAM98440
32. Correct Answer: A
Explanation/Reference:
Reference https://chaitanyaidm.wordpress.com/category/oag/oim/
33. Correct Answer: BD
34. Correct Answer: A
Explanation/Reference:
Reference
https://docs.oracle.com/cd/E27559_01/admin.1112/e27149/audit.htm#OMADM4758 (see note)
35. Correct Answer: AB
Explanation/Reference:
Reference
https://docs.oracle.com/cd/E27559_01/integration.1112/e27123/oid_oim.htm#IDMIG4358
36. Correct Answer: ABE
Explanation/Reference:

Reference
https://docs.oracle.com/cd/E21764_01/doc.1111/e14309/dcintro.ht
m#OMDEV2433 (1.6.5)
37. Correct Answer: B
38. Correct Answer: B
Explanation/Reference:
Reference
https://docs.oracle.com/cd/E27559_01/relnotes.1112/e35820/id_m
gr.htm#ASIRN4694
39. Correct Answer: D
40. Correct Answer: B
41. Correct Answer: A
Explanation/Reference:
Reference
https://docs.oracle.com/cd/E52734_01/oim/OMADM/system_props
.htm#OMADM884
42. Correct Answer: B
43. Correct Answer: A
44. Correct Answer: D